COLOUR ALONG WITH ME: MECHANICAL MENAGERIE

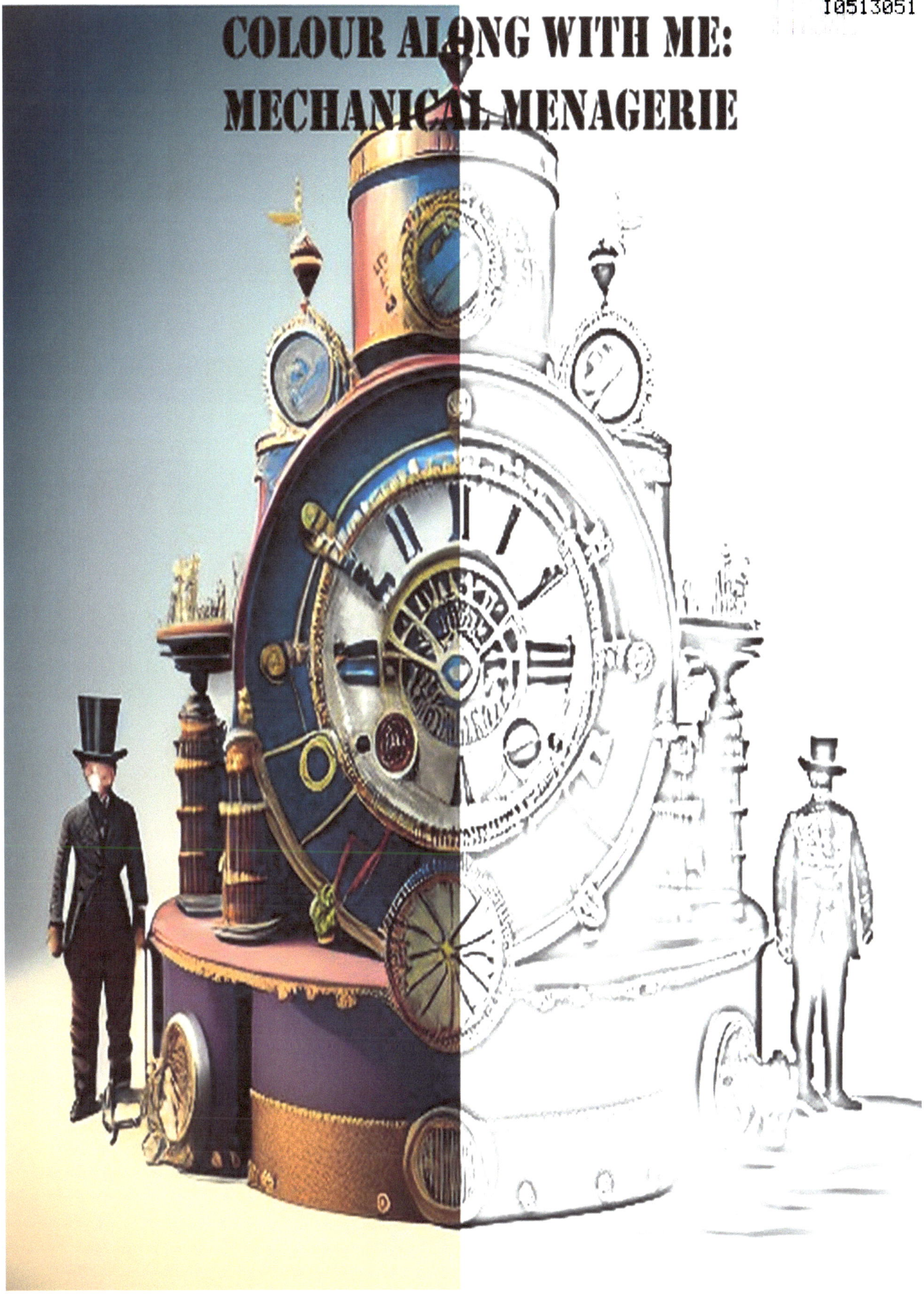

For my son and all the other aspiring artists out there, keep your pencils sharp and your mind sharper.

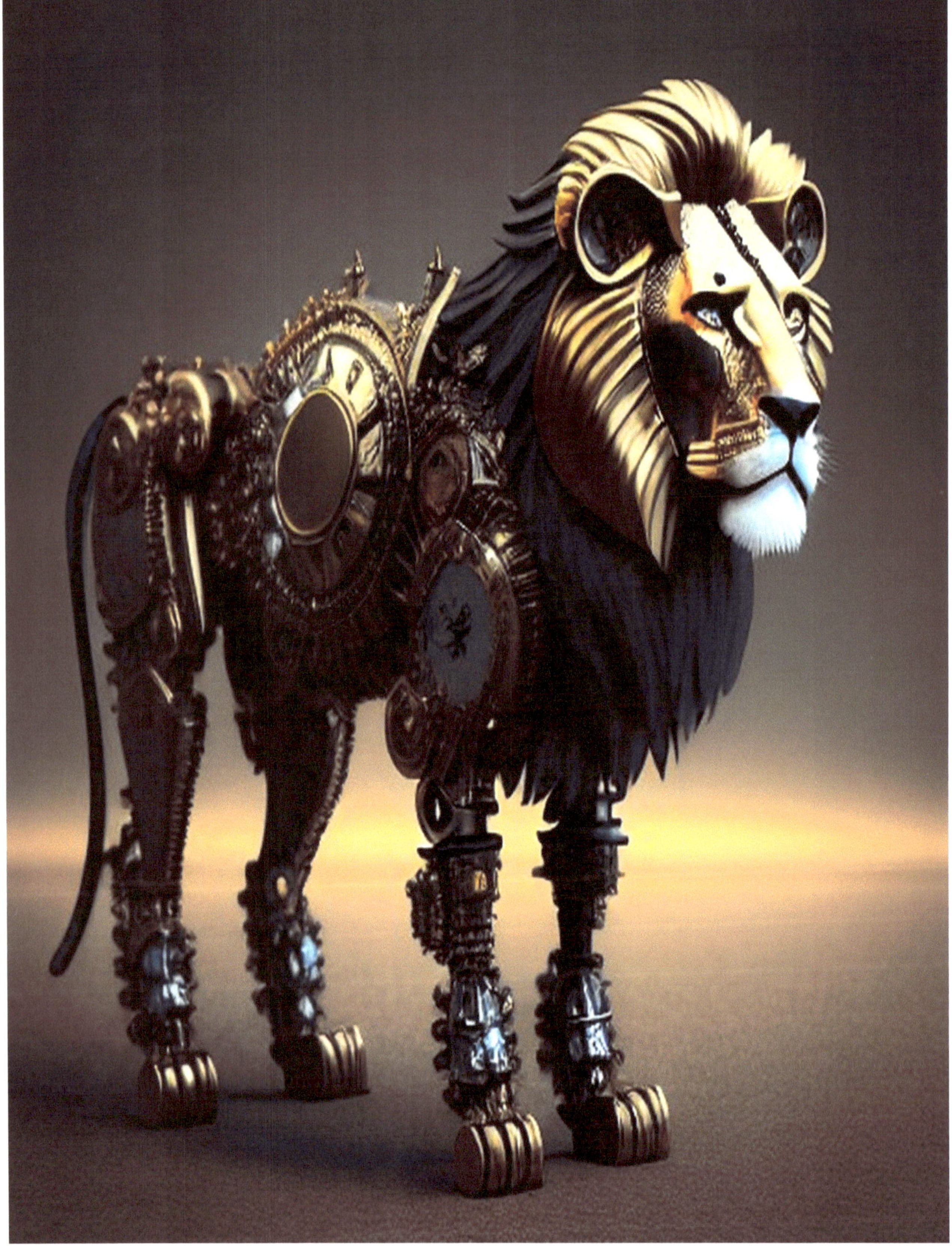

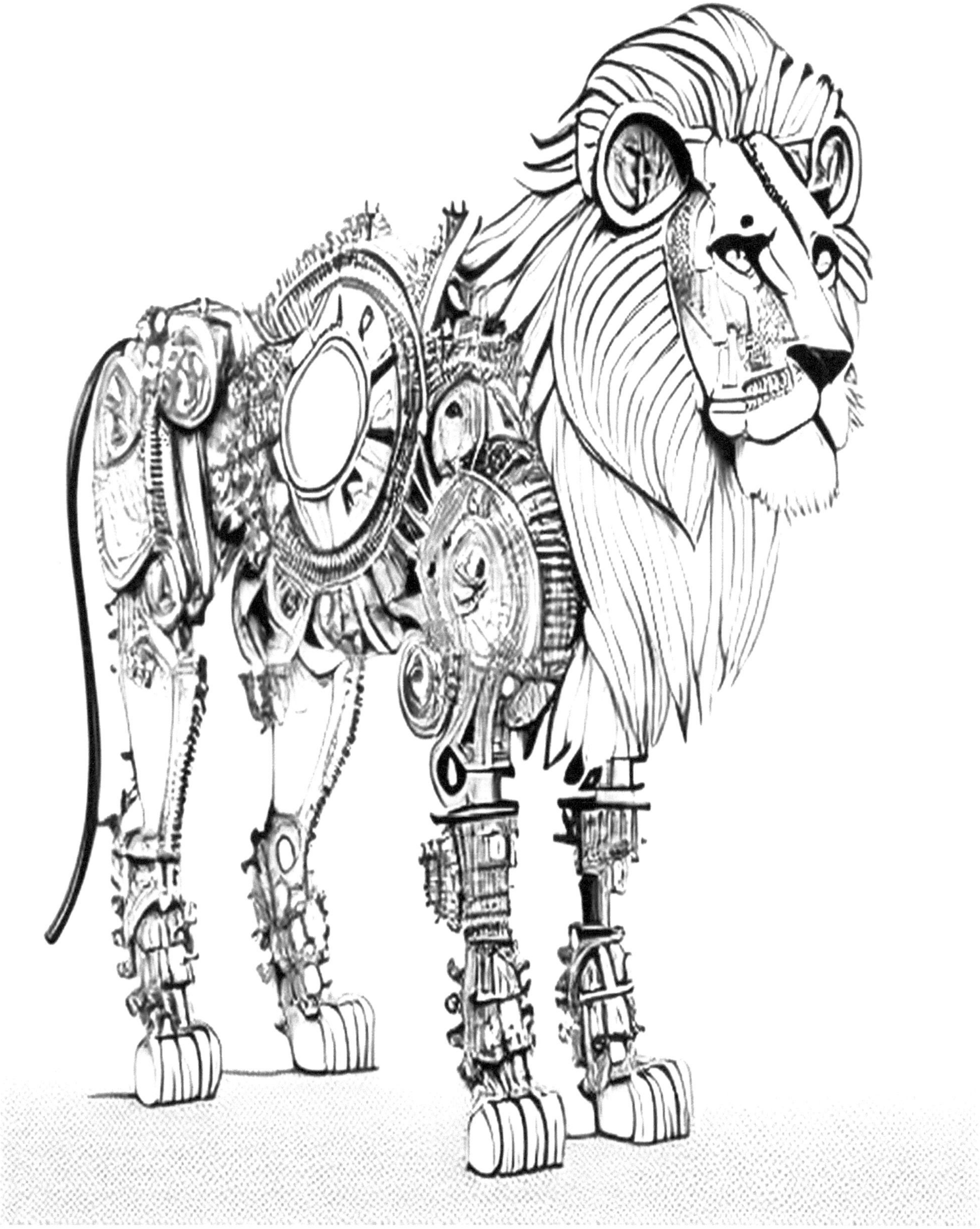

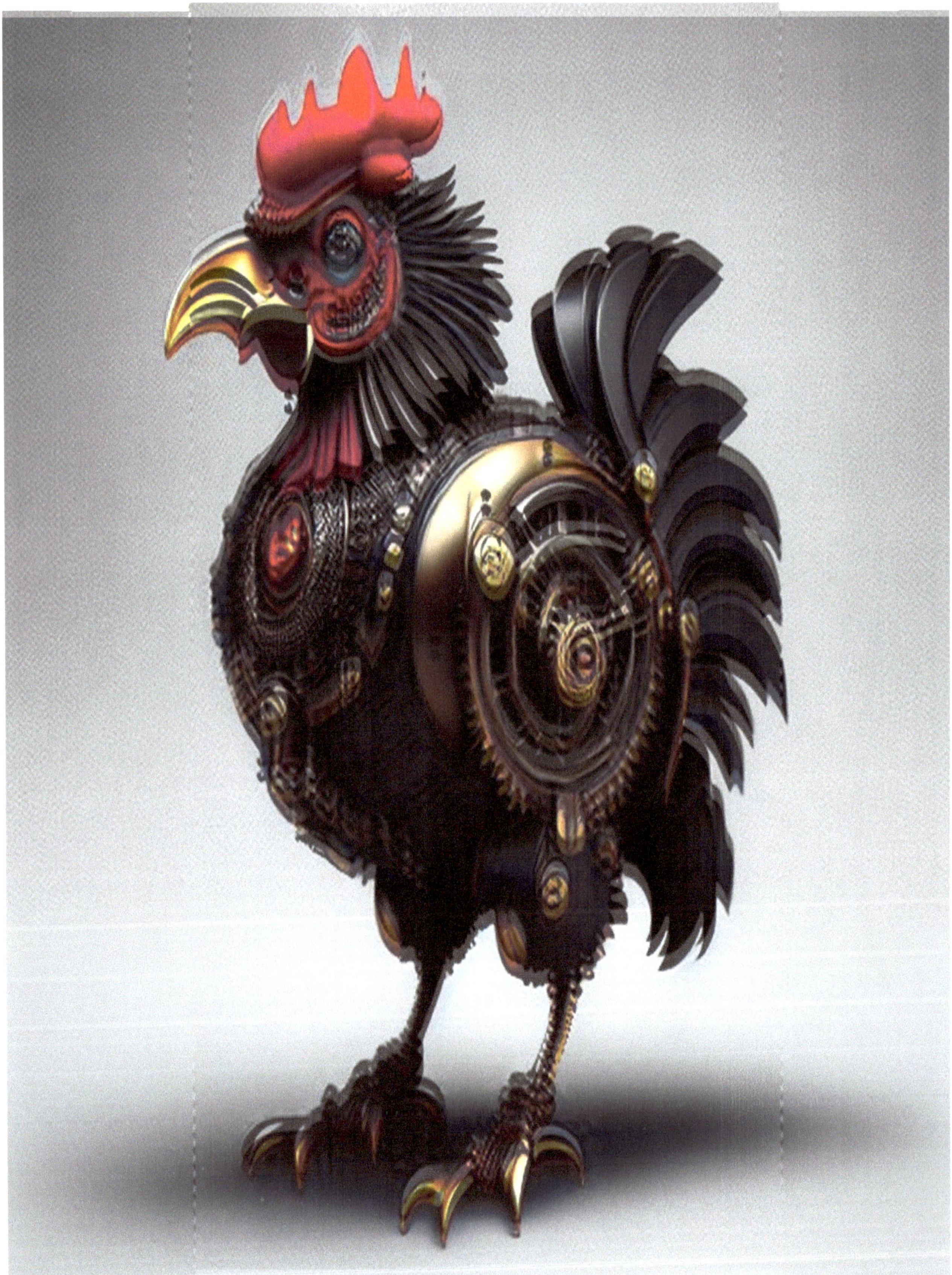

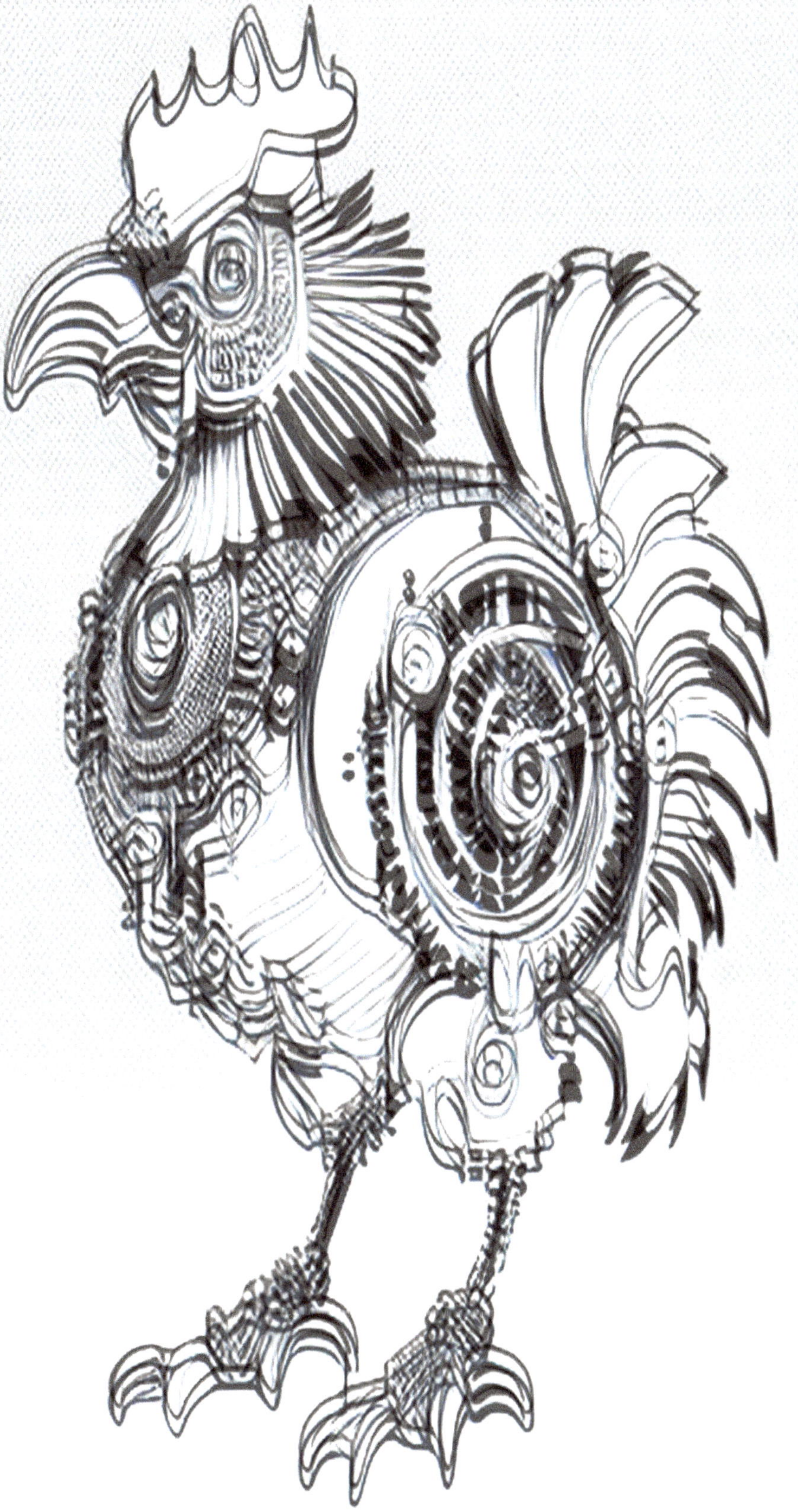

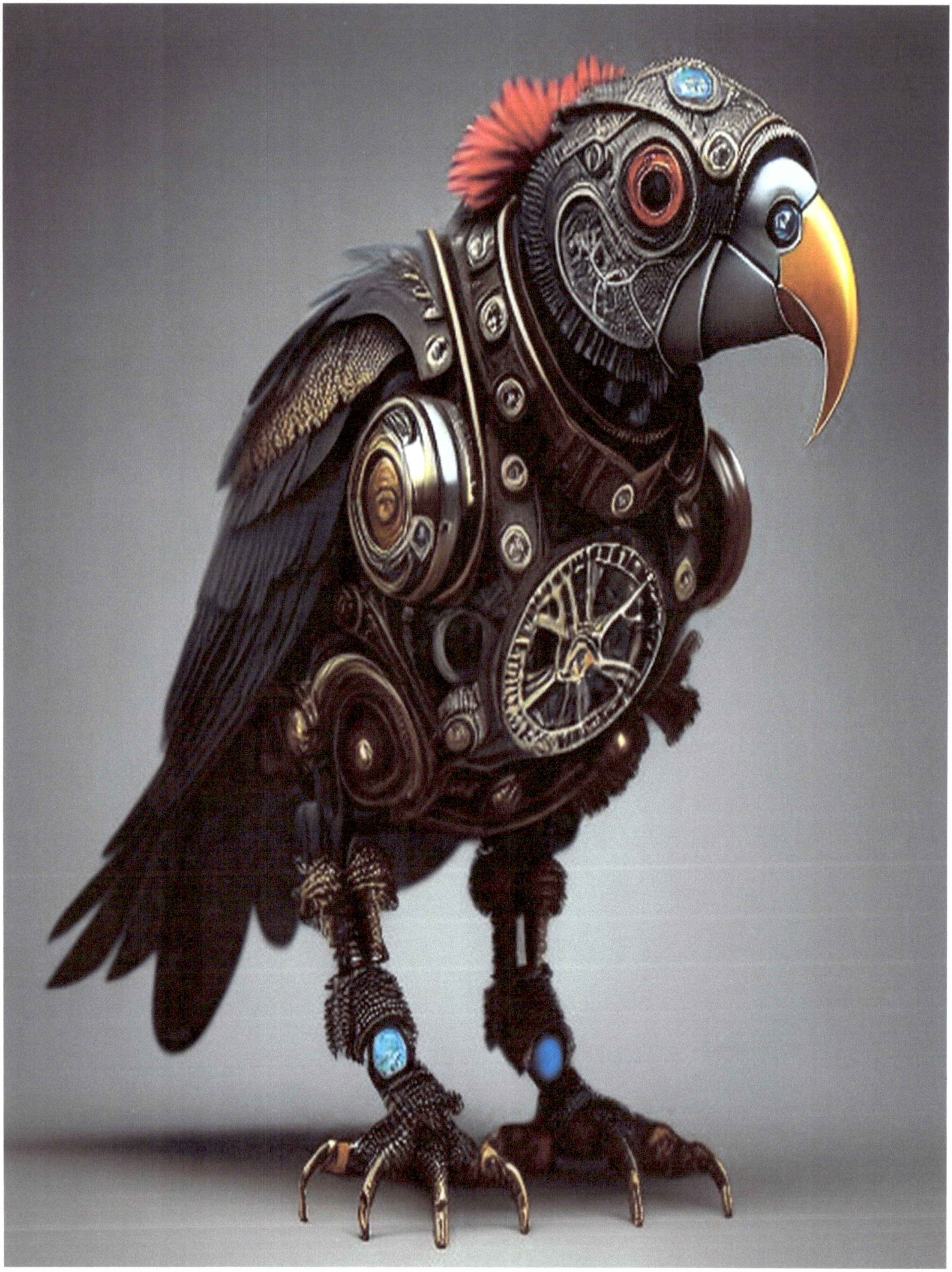

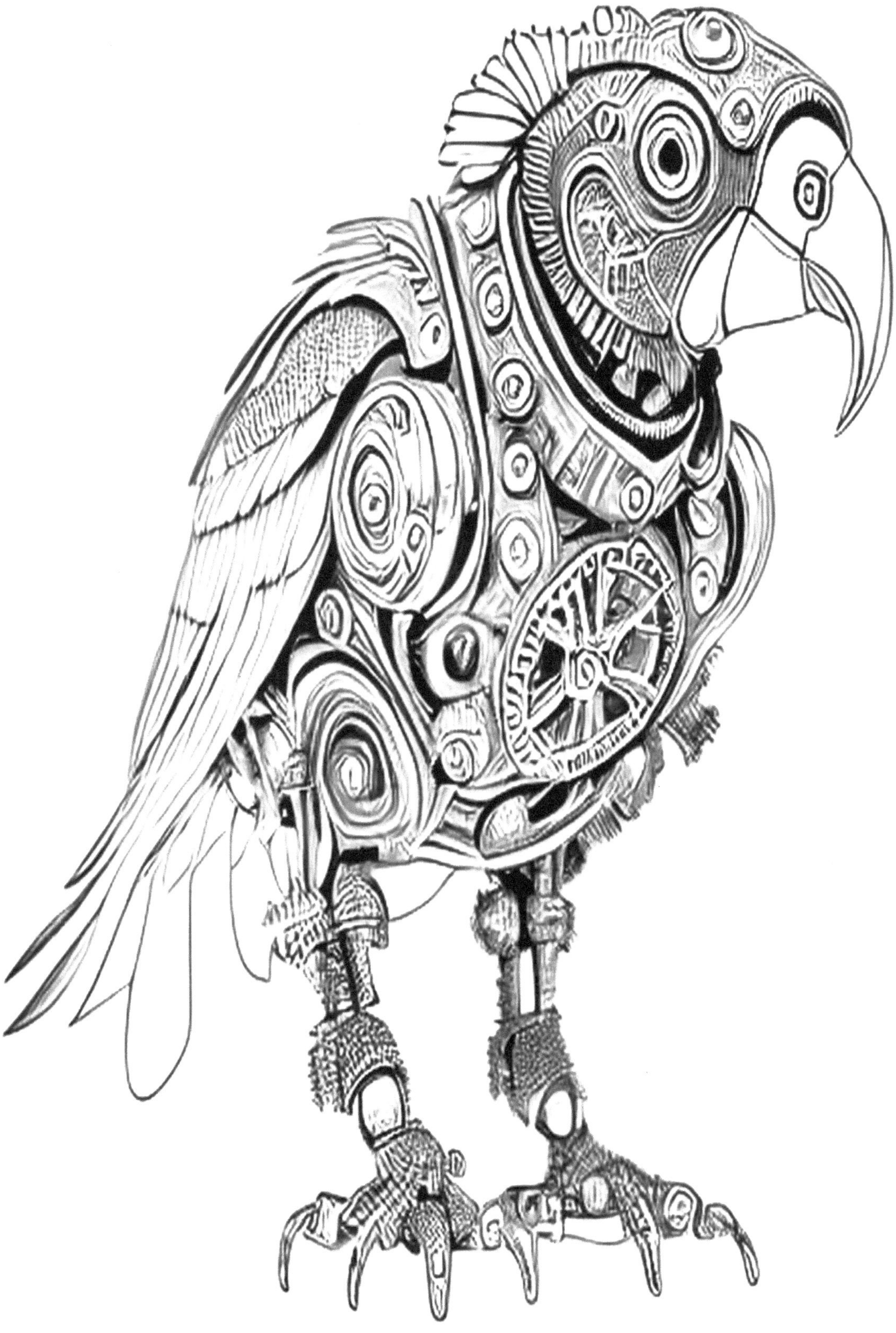

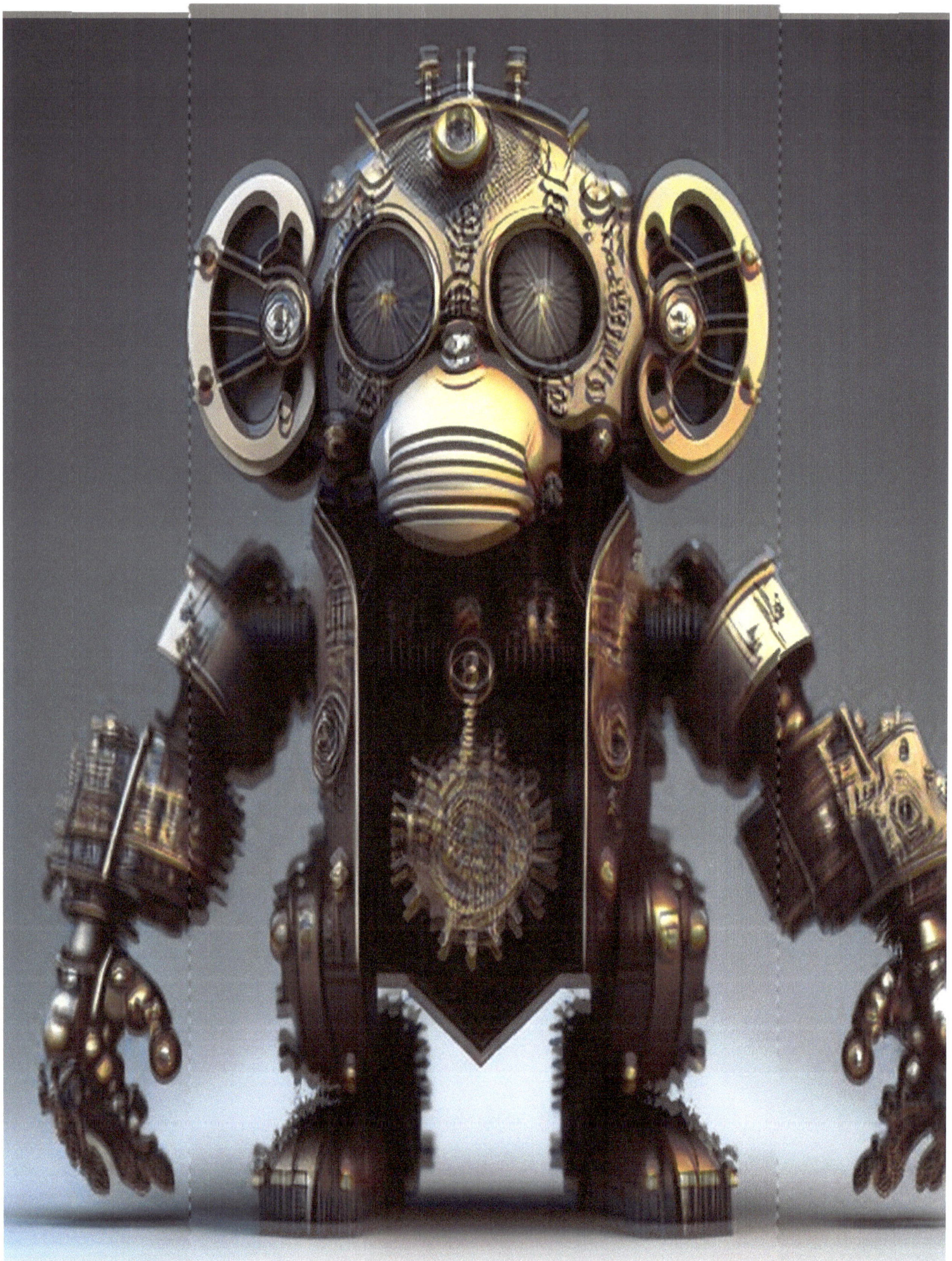

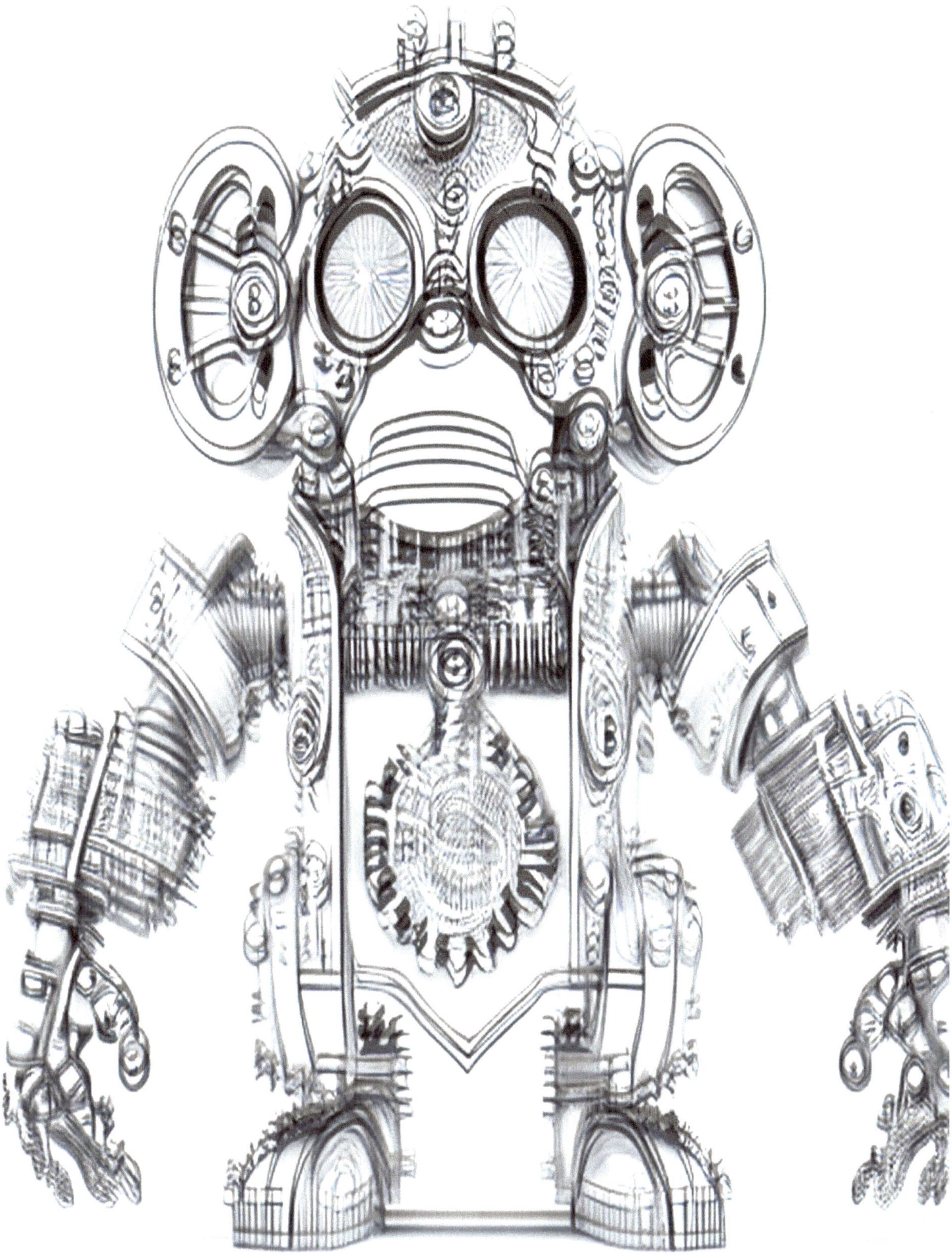

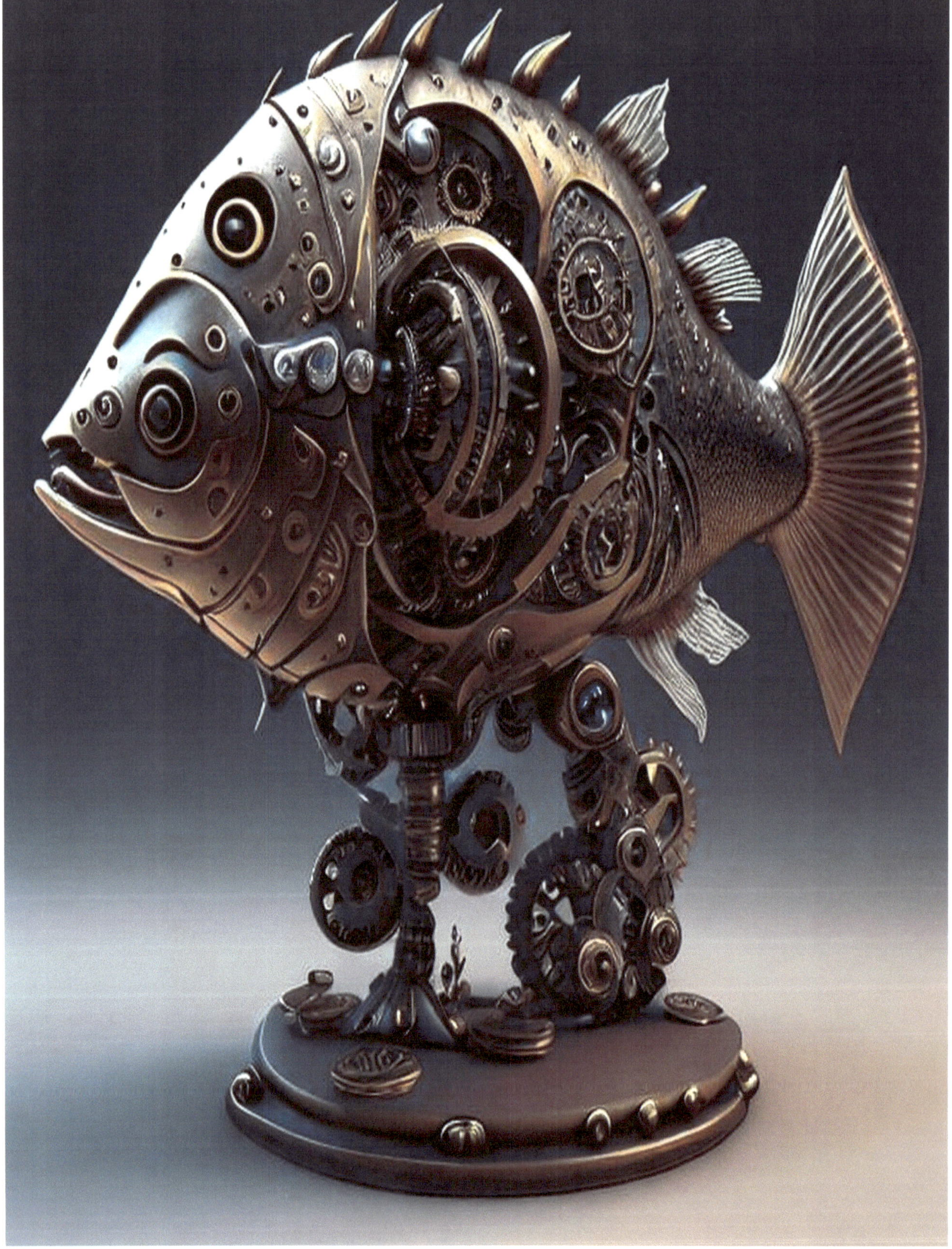

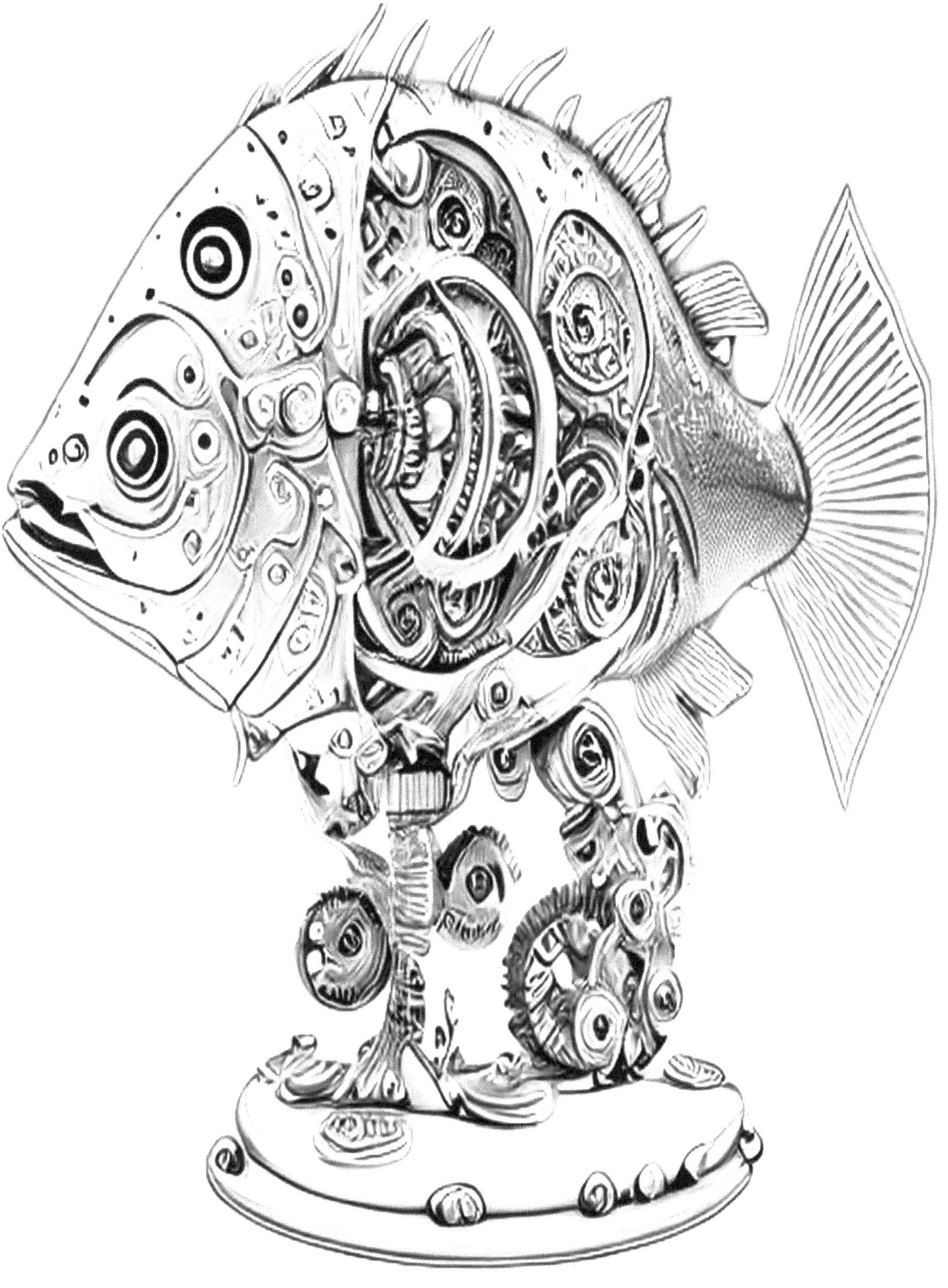

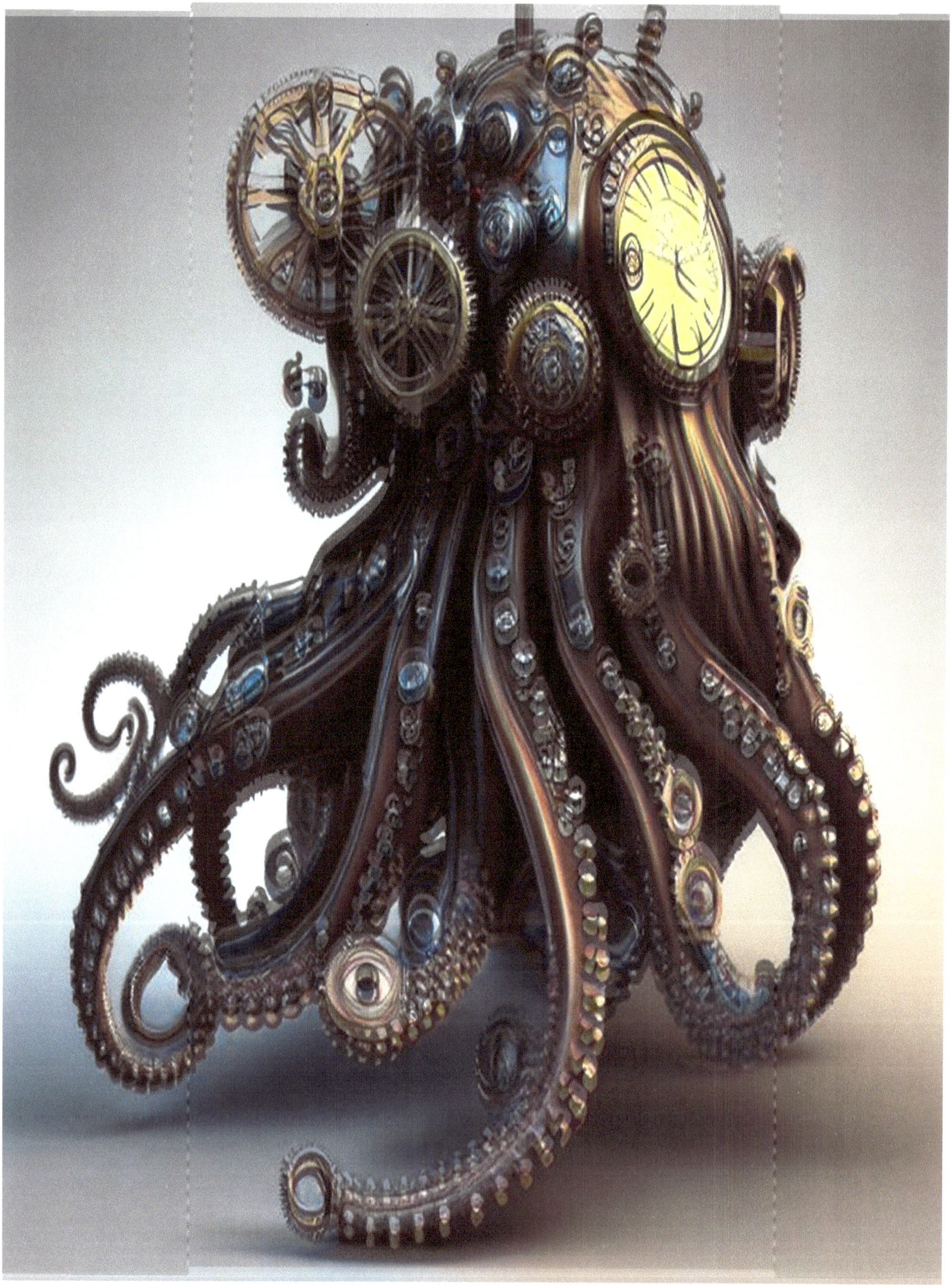

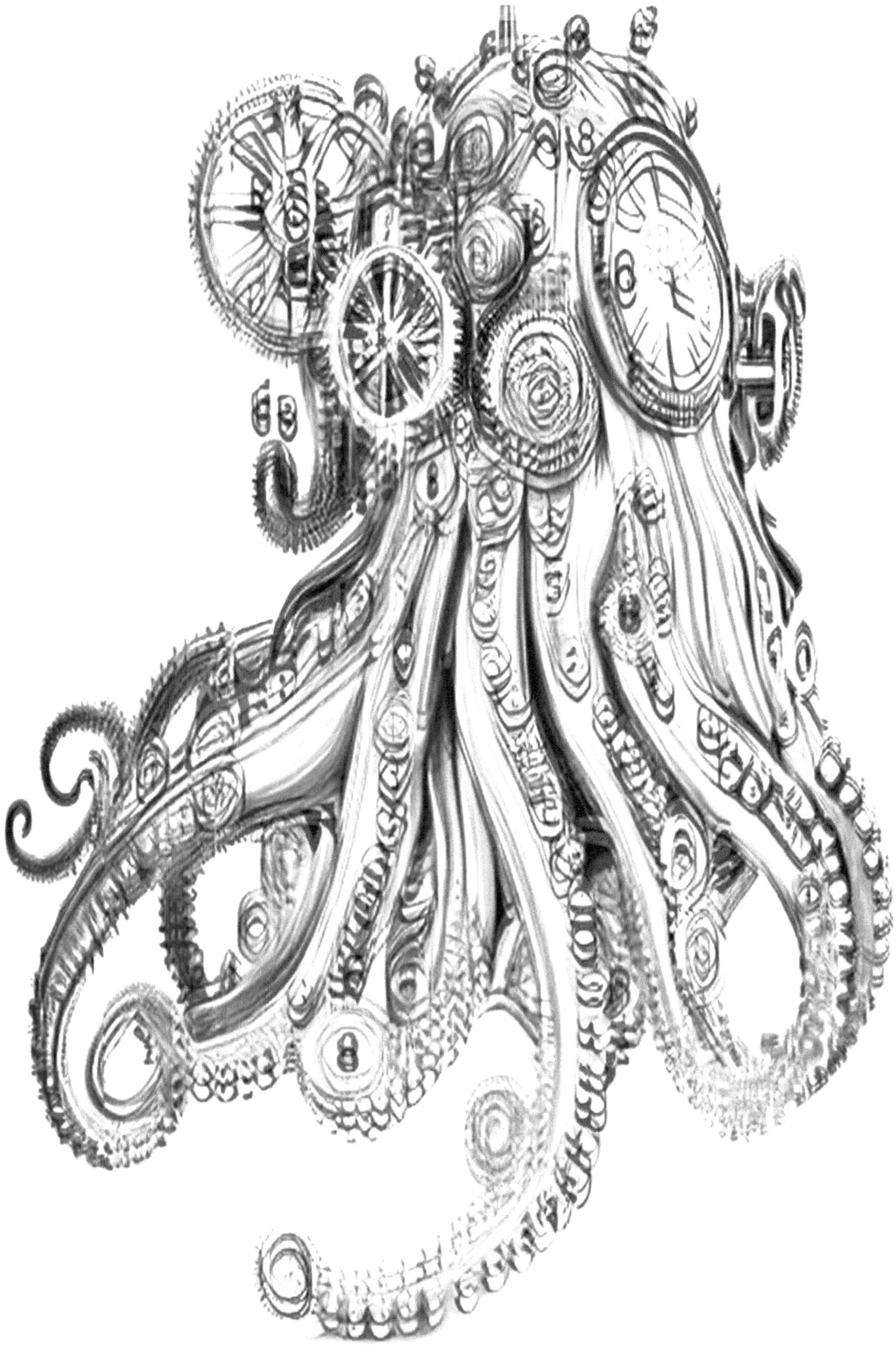

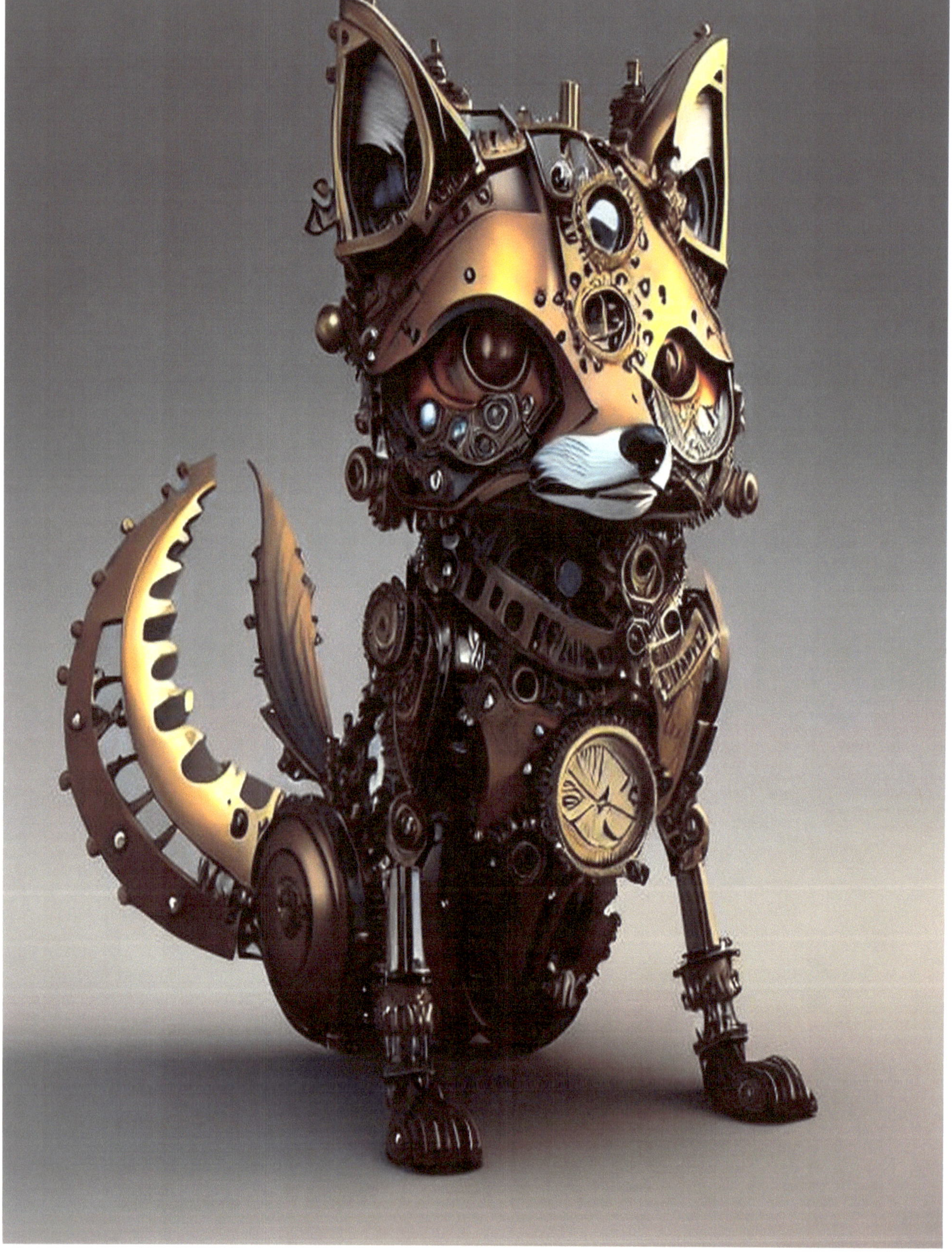

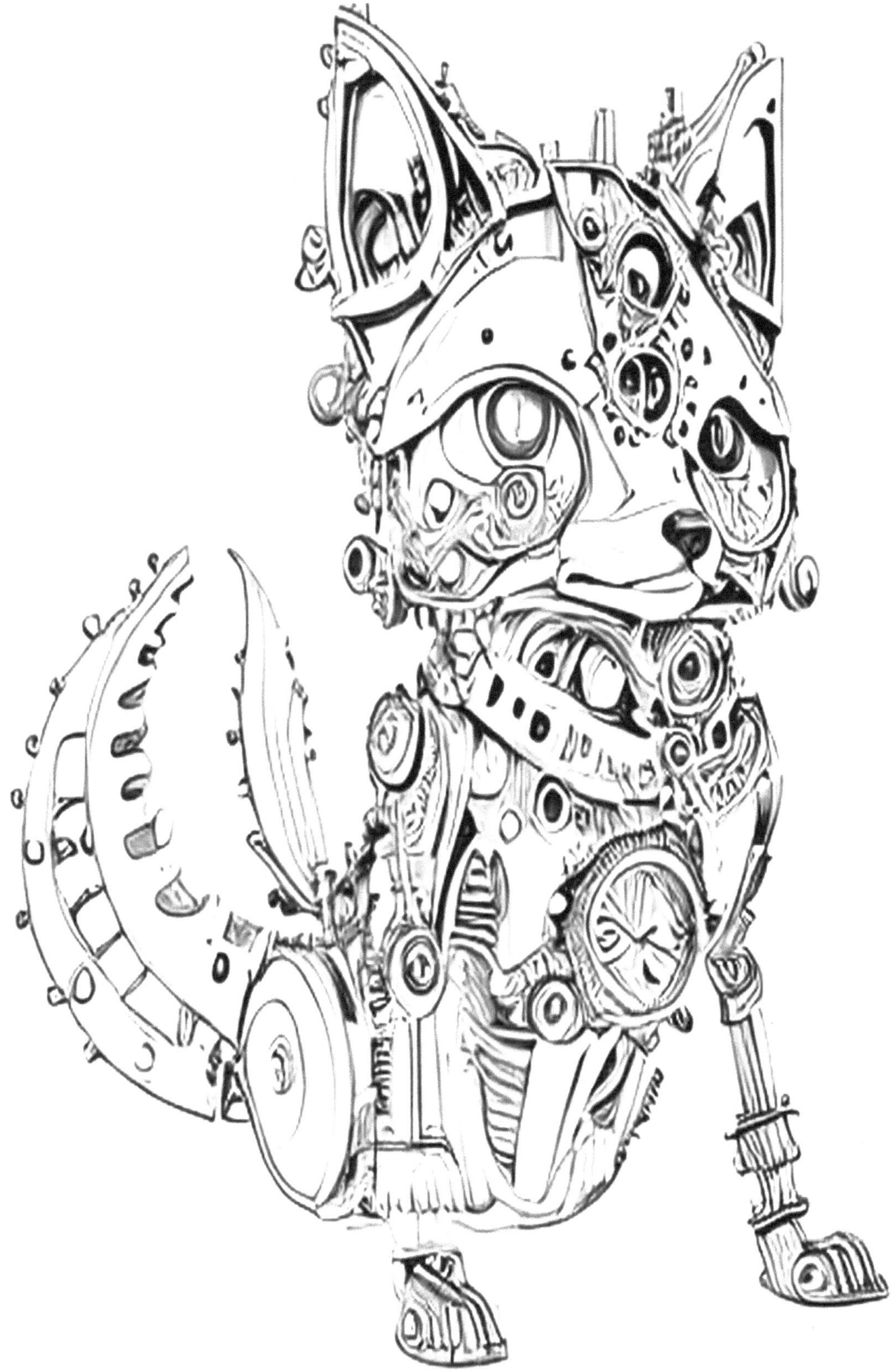

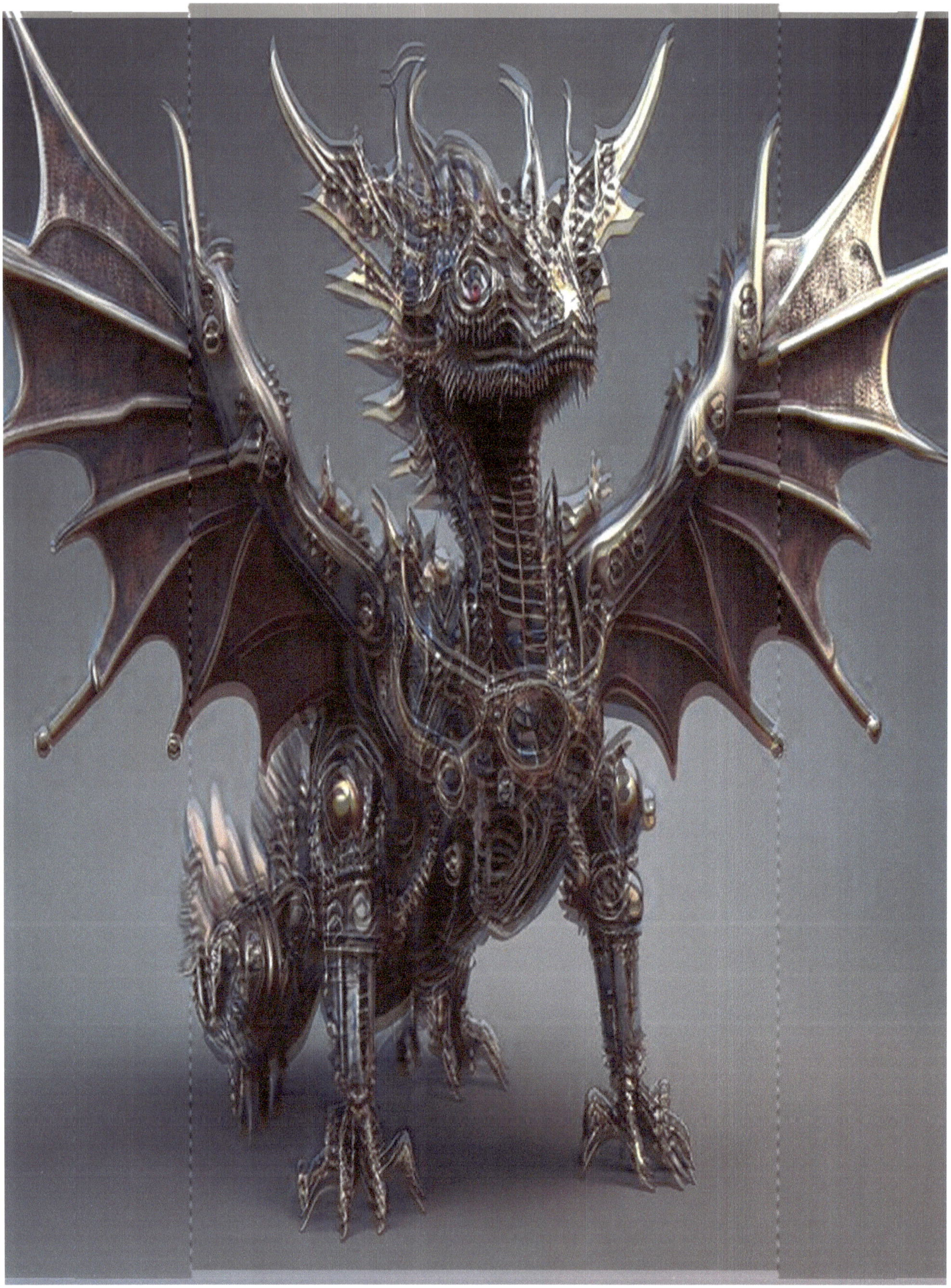

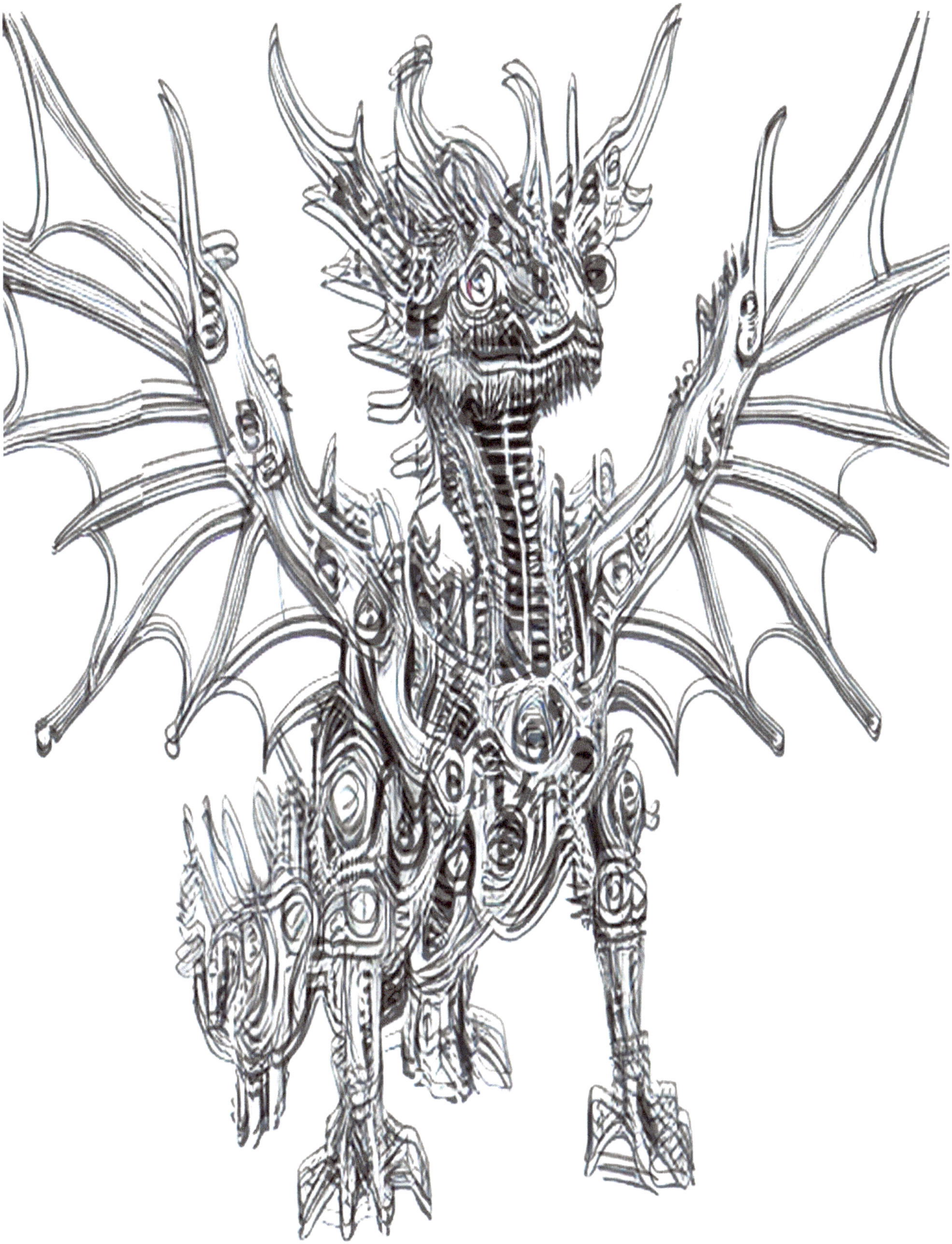

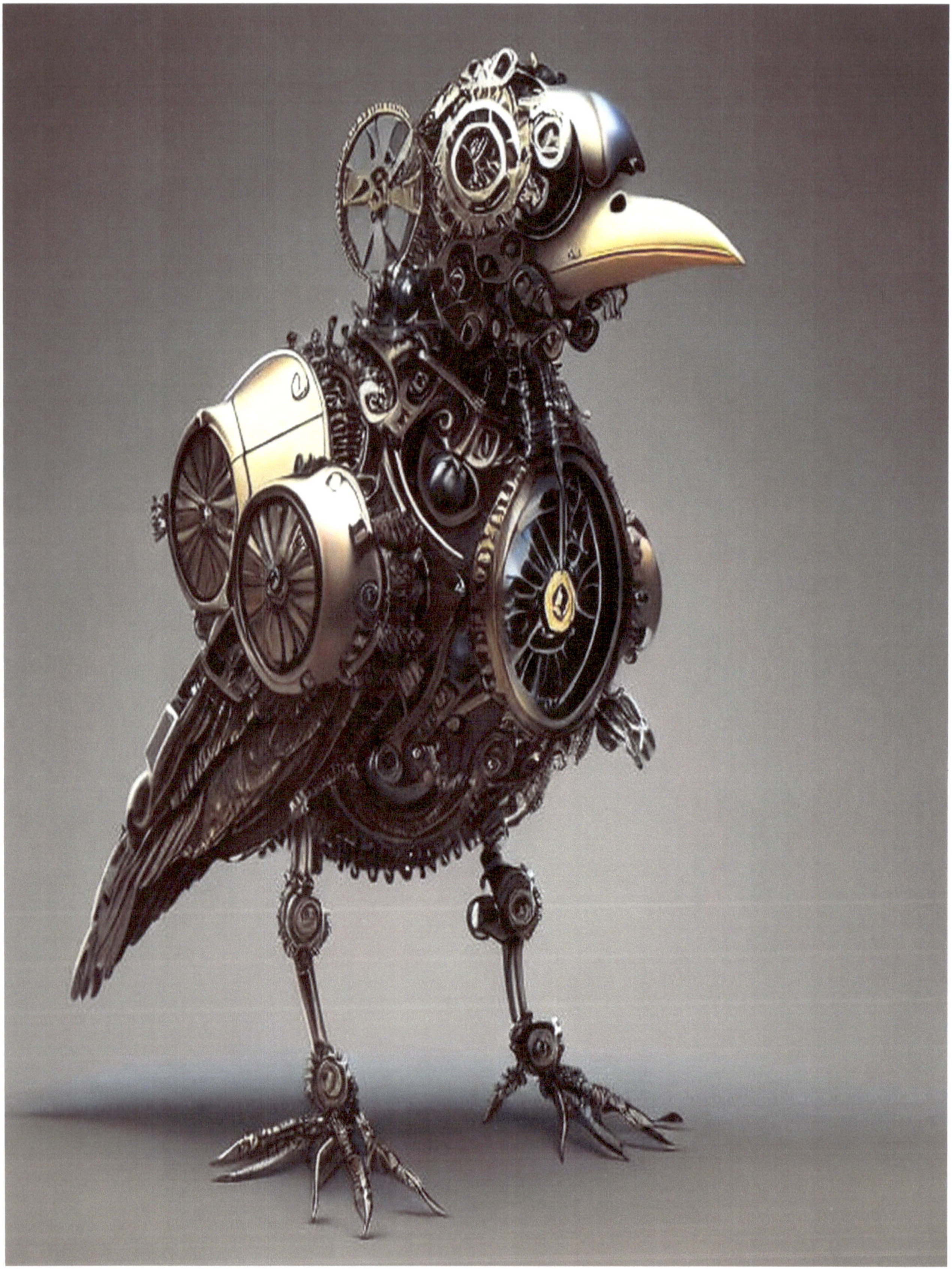

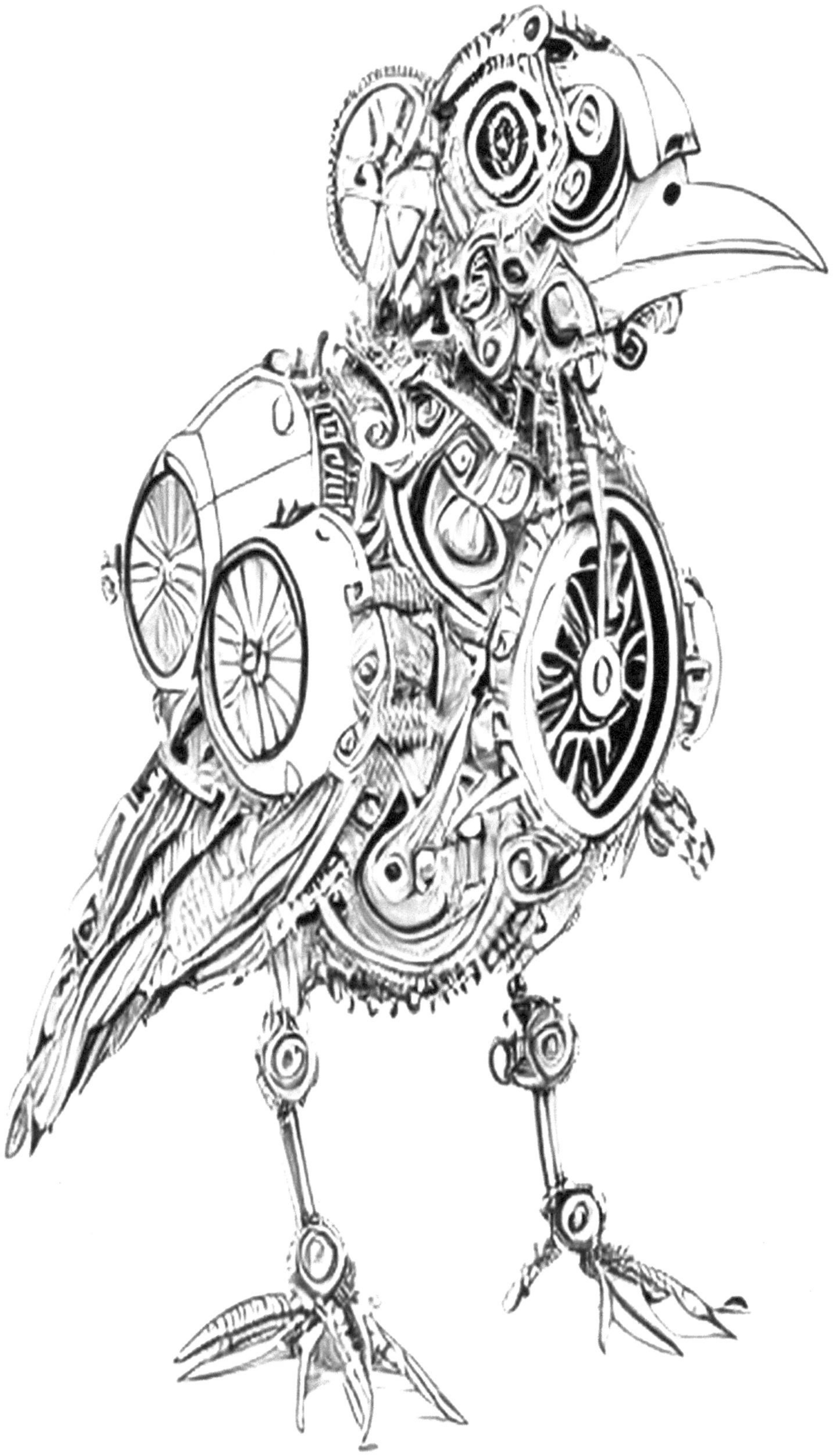

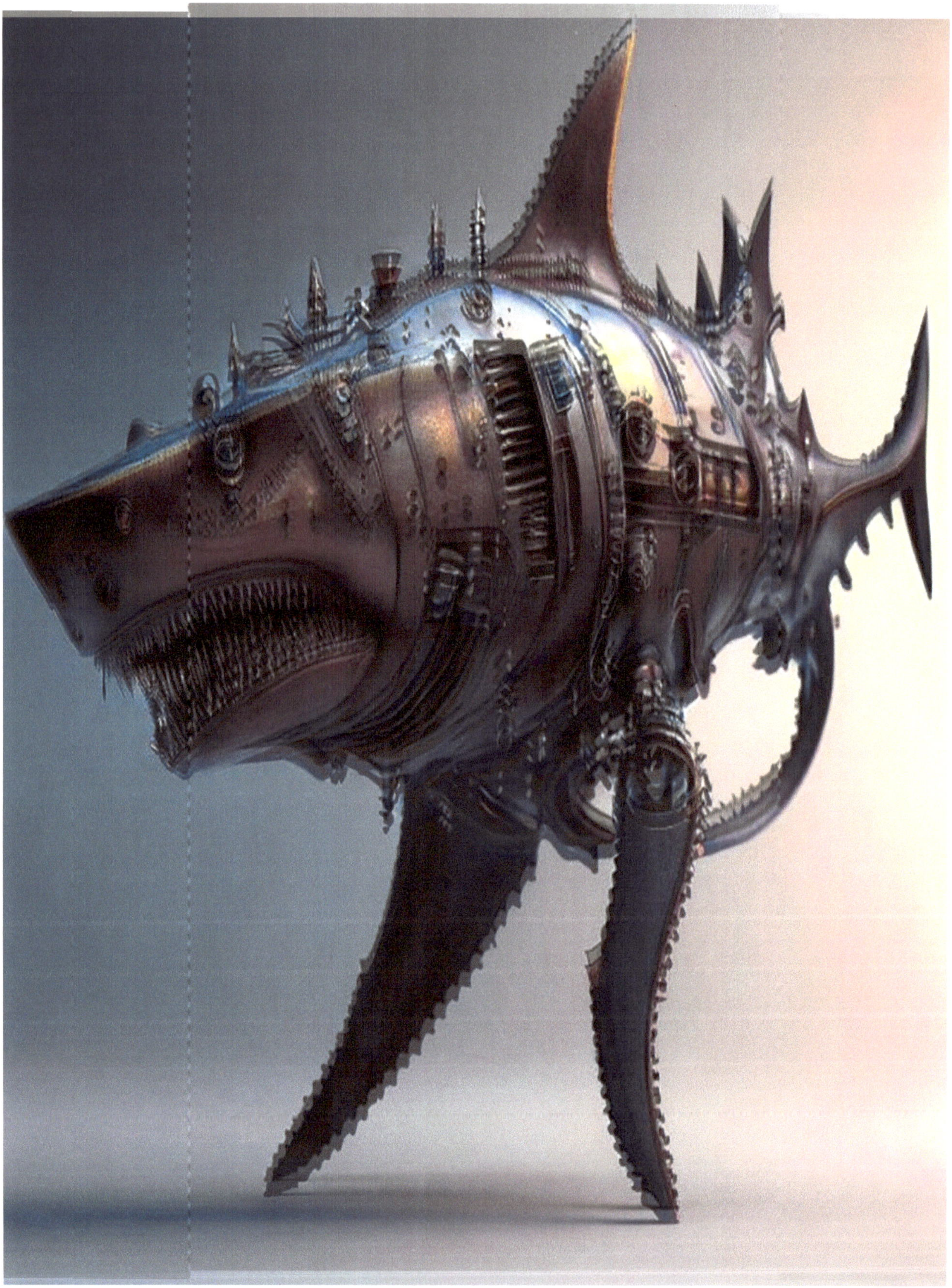

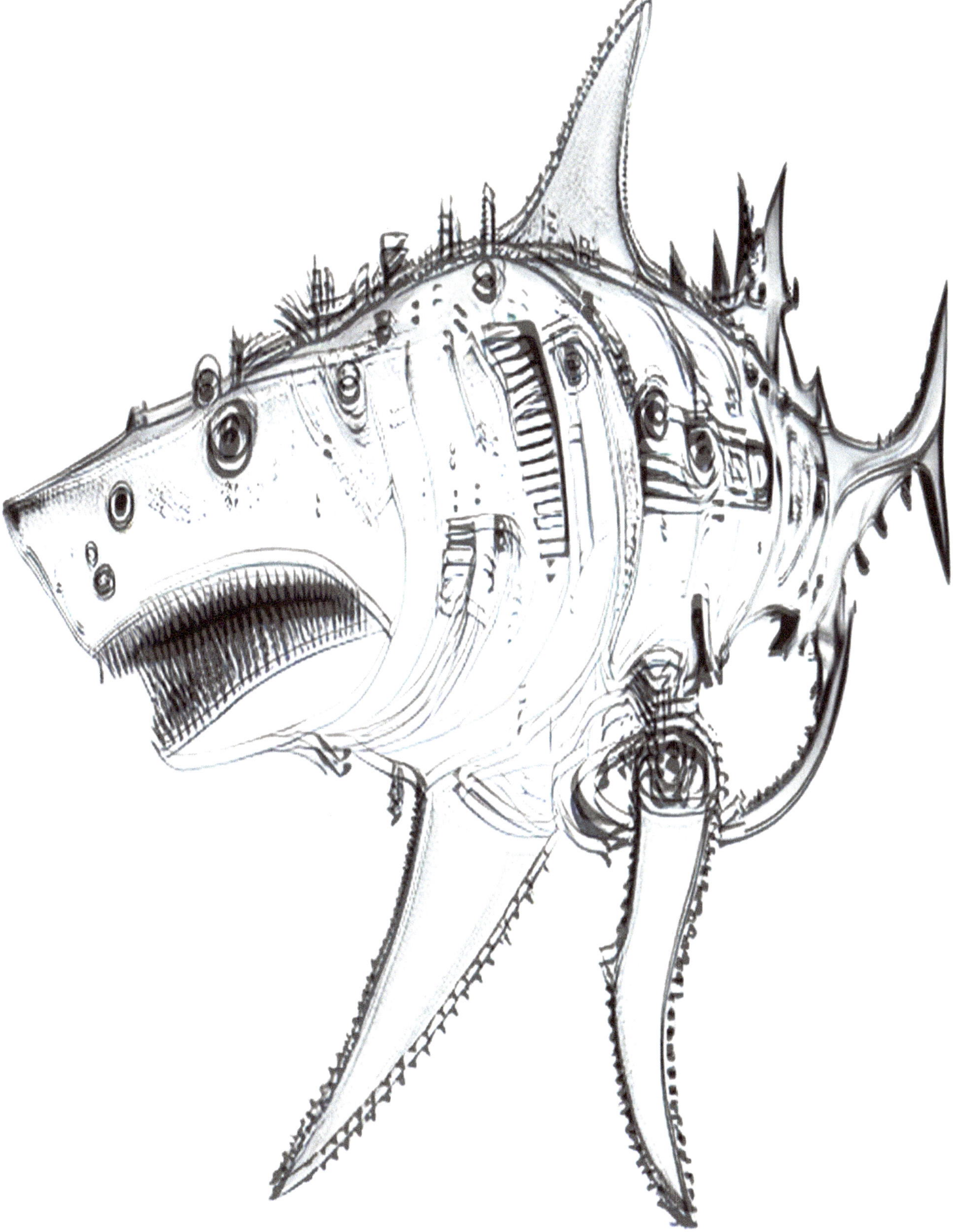

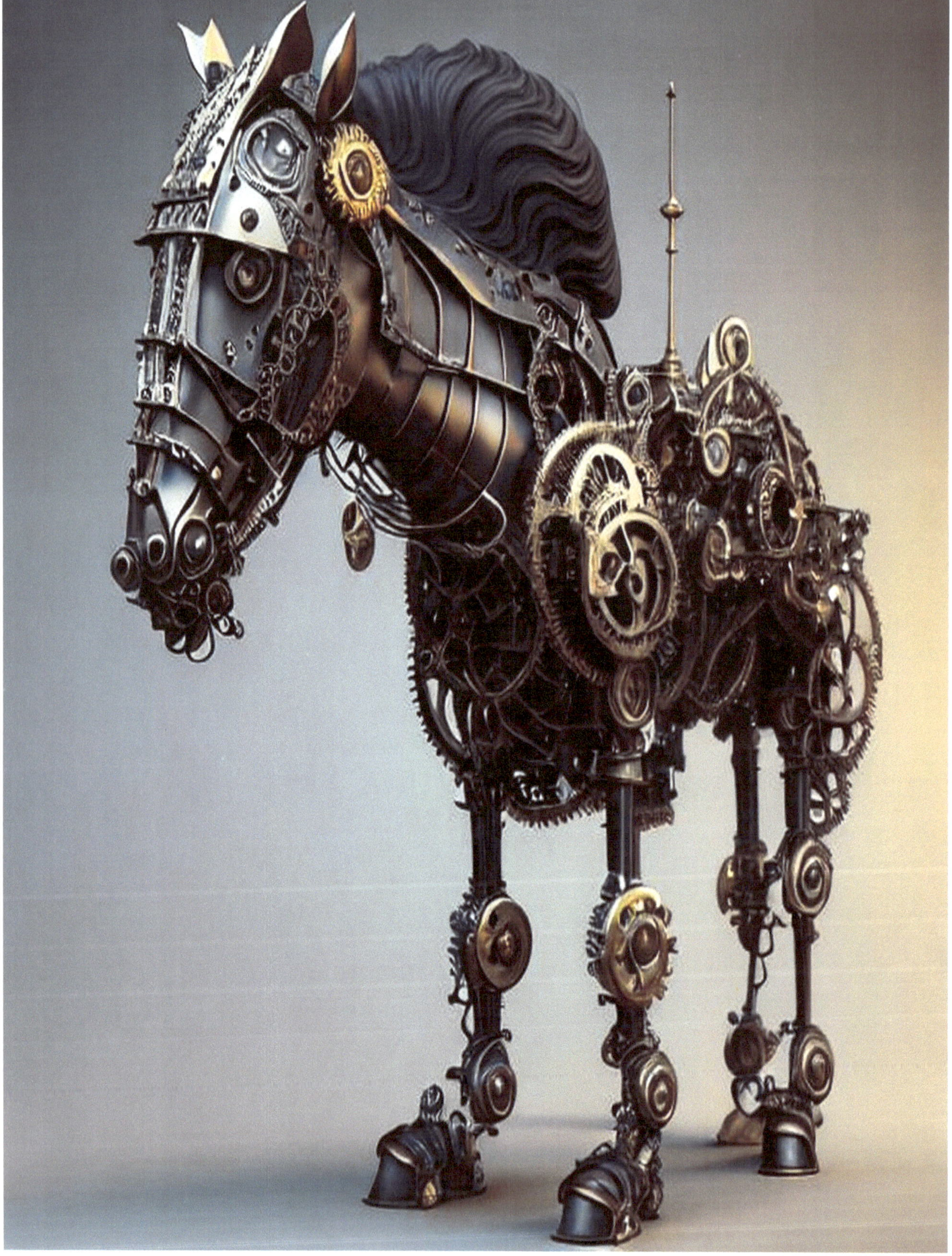

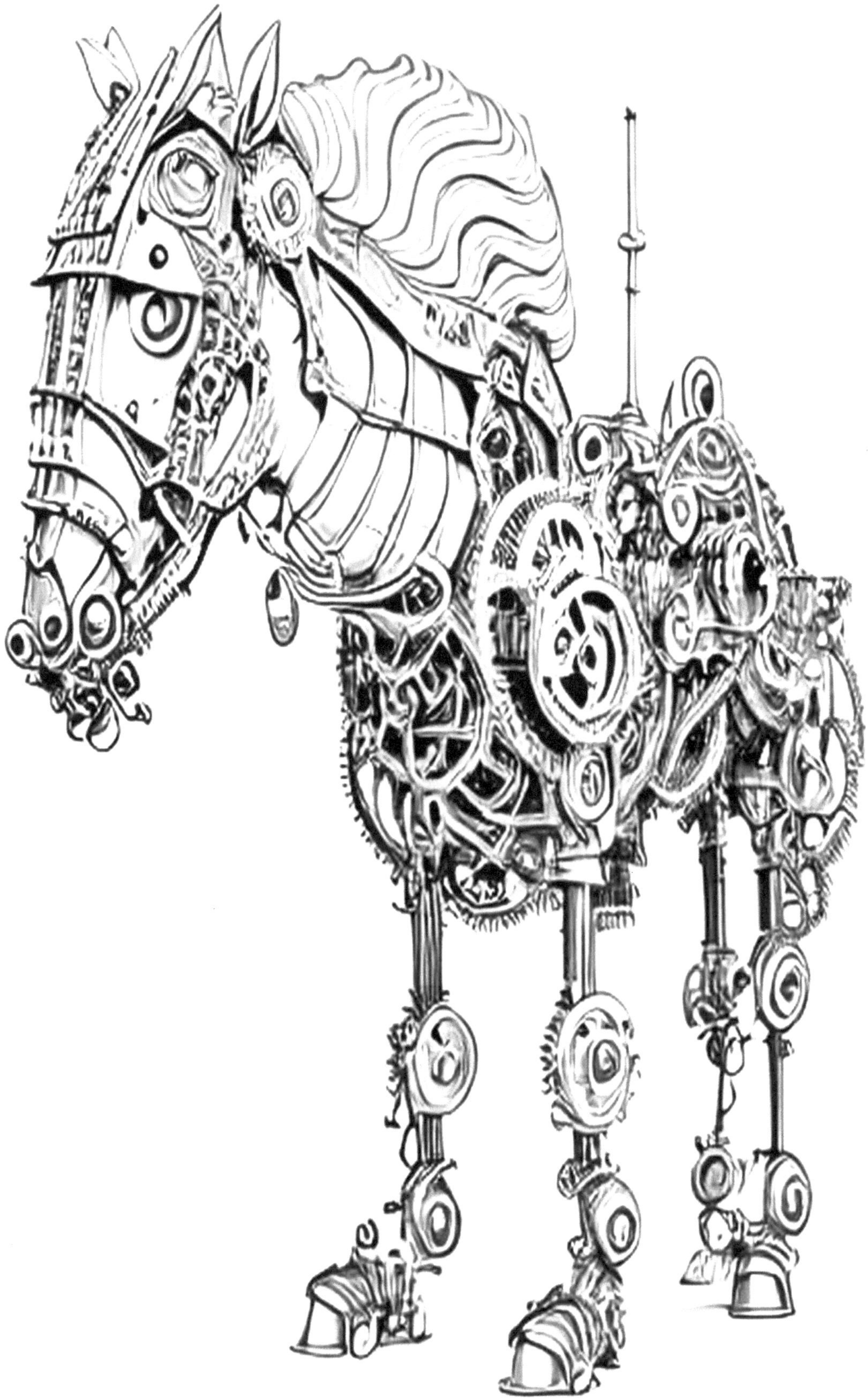